FEROCIOUS FIGHTING ANIMALS

WOLVERINES

Julia J. Quinlan

PowerKiDS
press

New York

Published in 2013 by The Rosen Publishing Group, Inc.
29 East 21st Street, New York, NY 10010

First Edition

Editor: Amelie von Zumbusch
Book Design: Andrew Povolny

Photo Credits: Cover S. J. Krasemann/Peter Arnold/Getty Images; p. 4 Daniel J Cox/Oxford Scientific/Getty Images; p. 5 Visceralimage/Shutterstock.com; p. 6 dotweb/Shutterstock.com; p. 7 (top) iStockphoto/Thinkstock; p. 7 (bottom) © iStockphoto/Justin Krall; pp. 8–9 Raimund Linke/Photodisc/Getty Images; p. 10 Juan Carlos Munoz/age fotostock/Getty Images; p. 11 Paul Oomen/Photographer's Choice/Getty Images; pp. 12–13 Jorgen Larsson/Nordic Photos/Getty Images; p. 14 AP Photo/The News Tribune/Lui Kit Wong; p. 15 Daniel Cox/Oxford Scientific/Getty Images; pp. 16–17 Thomas Kitchin & Victoria Hurst/All Canada Photos/Getty Images; p. 18 Stockbyte/Thinkstock; p. 19 Hemera/Thinkstock; p. 20 Geoffrey Kuchera/Shutterstock.com; p. 21 Tiffany Rose/WireImage/Getty Images; p. 22 Jeremy Woodhouse/Photodisc/Getty Images.

Library of Congress Cataloging-in-Publication Data

Quinlan, Julia J.
  Wolverines / by Julia J. Quinlan. — 1st ed.
    p. cm. — (Ferocious fighting animals)
Includes index.
ISBN 978-1-4488-9672-1 (library binding) — ISBN 978-1-4488-9802-2 (pbk.) —
ISBN 978-1-4488-9803-9 (6-pack)
1. Wolverine—Juvenile literature. I. Title.
QL737.C25Q46 2013
599.766—dc23

                                        2012027023

Manufactured in United States of America

CPSIA Compliance Information: Batch #W13PK5: For Further Information contact Rosen Publishing, New York, New York at 1-800-237-9932

CONTENTS

MEET THE WOLVERINE

Wolverines are related to weasels and martens but look more like small bears. Though they are fairly small and very furry, they are not friendly or cuddly. They are ferocious predators! They are able to kill prey many times their size, such as caribou.

A wolverine's teeth are very sharp. They can cut through bones and frozen meat!

Wolverines love to hunt and eat. They are also known as gluttons. A glutton is a person or animal that eats a lot. Wolverines are so fearsome that sometimes they do not even have to fight other animals, they can just scare them away. Wolverines are so tough that they have been known to scare away bears!

Wolverines have webbed feet that act like snowshoes and allow them to run quickly on mounds of snow.

FURRY FIGHTERS

Wolverines are fairly short but have long bodies. Males can grow to be 4 feet (1 m) long and 18 inches (46 cm) tall. They can weigh up to 66 pounds (30 kg). Female wolverines are generally smaller and lighter. Wolverines have bushy tails that are 5 to 10 inches (13–25 cm) long.

Wolverines have an incredibly strong sense of smell. They can find bodies that were buried under 20 feet (6 m) of snow!

Wolverines have dark brown fur with two lighter brown stripes starting at their necks going down to their tails. They have very strong teeth that can bite through bone. They have long sharp claws that they use for fighting and digging. Wolverines have **glands** that give off an unpleasant smell.

Wolverines' sharp, curved claws help them climb on ice and up cliffs.

Wolverines make unusually deep growls for animals of their size.

SNOWY HOMES

Wolverines live in many countries, including the United States, Canada, Russia, and Finland. They live in the cold, northern parts of these countries. They also live in high mountains with cold **climates**. Some live in forests, but others live in places where trees cannot grow. Wolverines like snowy areas. They prey on animals that get stuck in snowdrifts and **avalanches**.

Wolverines generally do not dig their own burrows. Instead, they find shelter just about anywhere. Sometimes they will sleep in burrows made by other animals. Wolverines do not have permanent homes. However, female wolverines dig temporary burrows in which to give birth.

Unlike many animals that live in cold places, wolverines do not hibernate. They are active even during the snowiest weather.

HUGE HOME RANGES

Wolverines live alone for the most part. They are often **nocturnal**, or most active at night. Some wolverines live very far north, in places where during parts of the year there are 24 hours of sunlight. During those times, wolverines are active even though it is light out.

Wolverines are good at climbing trees. They run and swim well, too.

Wolverines may travel 15 miles (24 km) in a day while looking for food.

Wolverines have huge **home ranges**. These are the areas where wolverines live and hunt. Wolverines' home ranges tend to measure between 38 square miles (100 sq km) and 230 square miles (600 sq km). Male wolverines use their scent glands to mark their home ranges. A male's home range often overlaps with those of several females.

FEROCIOUS WOLVERINES

Wolverines are known for their strength and willingness to fight. They will attack injured lynx. They have been known to steal food from polar bears, mountain lions, and packs of wolves. They fight other wolverines of the same sex that enter their home ranges.

BABY WOLVERINES

The only time wolverines come together is during **mating** season, when they make babies. The mating season lasts from April until August. Wolverine babies are usually born in February or March. Baby wolverines are called kits.

This wolverine kit is a day old. As you can see, newborn kits have white fur.

Kits drink their mothers' milk for the first 8 to 10 weeks.

Female wolverines usually have two or three kits at a time. Occasionally they will have four. Kits are born with thick fur. They drink milk from their mothers. Young wolverines stay with their mothers for up to two years before they start living on their own. Wolverines in the wild usually live for 7 to 12 years. Wolverines in **captivity** have lived up to 20 years.

FIERCE PREDATORS

Wolverines are **omnivores**, but they eat mostly meat. They are smart and have many ways to get food. They often eat prey killed by other animals. To get this premade meal, a wolverine shows its teeth, sticks up its tail, and growls at the other predator. Wolverines look so ferocious that the other predator tends to run away rather than fight!

Wolverines can take down caribou and other large mammals that have gotten stuck in deep snow. If a wolverine cannot finish its meal, it will use its scent glands to mark the prey so that other animals do not eat it.

Wolverines will feed on animals that have died due to injuries or harsh weather conditions.

THREATS TO WOLVERINES

Wolverines do not have many natural predators. Because they are so ferocious, few animals try to hunt them. However, mountain lions, wolves, and bears sometimes kill wolverines. Wolverines do not go down without a fight, though. They will try to scare

Wolverines sometimes follow wolves in order to eat their leftovers. If the wolf spots a wolverine, the two will fight.

In the past, trappers prized wolverine fur and often used it to line the hoods of their coats.

away larger predators by growling at them. If they cannot scare them, they will try to fight them off.

Humans are the main threat to wolverines. Wolverines are hunted for their fur. They were hunted almost to **extinction** in the nineteenth century. Luckily, wolverines have made a comeback in many areas. However, farmers still sometimes kill wolverines because they eat farm animals.

HUMANS AND WOLVERINES

Besides being hunted by humans, wolverines are also harmed by human activities. **Deforestation** harms wolverines. Fewer forests mean fewer places for wolverines to live. Wolverines are also affected

Wolverines live in places where there is snow on the ground during the spring. Global warming may make these places rarer.

by **global warming**. As the world gets warmer, there are fewer places that get the heavy snows that wolverines are used to.

Though some people hunt wolverines, others admire them for their toughness. Michigan is known as the Wolverine State, even though the state does not have a big wolverine **population** today. Wolverines are so fierce that a superhero is named after them! Wolverine the superhero is featured in the X-Men movies and comic books.

This is a statue of the superhero Wolverine as he appeared in several movies in the 2000s.

TOUGH SURVIVORS

It is hard for scientists to guess how big the wolverine population is. Wolverines are hard to find. This is because wolverines have such large ranges and mostly live alone. However, scientists do not consider them **endangered**. Wolverines have been driven out of some places due to deforestation and global warming. However, there are still many places where they can live.

Wolverines are tough and resourceful. Their ferociousness makes them successful predators, despite the harsh climates in which they live.

Some countries where wolverines were once heavily hunted now have laws protecting them.